the ocean

Illustrations by Kamilla Tolnø

ktolnoe.com

ISBN: 9788793972049

the ocean

the northern collection III

k. tolnoe

in the warm summer bliss
the air is standing still
yet everything is in motion
the world around you seems to change faster
than you do
there is a heaviness in your body
stuck on the bottom of the sea
praying for the light to touch you
for someone to understand
until the storm calms itself
and it's finally crystal clear
that there is no redemption
outside of yourself
only you can release the weights
of past versions of yourself
let the salt water rinse your soul
and clear you of the burdens
so that you can finally fly
underwater
and rise to the surface
to understand the extent
of our magnificent world
to look in the mirror
of the sky and the sun
to see that you now are
the ocean

we are waves
we are soft
yet destructive

coming and going
meeting and leaving

drifting in and out of lives
going low and going high

and when one goes
when one dies
a new one will come
to complete
this endless cycle of life

what are you
if not an ocean?
a liquid wilderness
in a soft firm form
salt and minerals
running in your veins
your eyes the only escape
a breath like waves
powerful in the softest of ways
a living mosaic of light and dark
of life and death
and blessed with a heart of mysteries
that most visitors
can only hope to see

i am homesick for a feeling
not a place

i am lying on the seabed
while heavy waves of nostalgia
come crashing in
drowning my rational thoughts
washing away my hopes and dreams
until all that i see
is what i have lost
i miss feeling like
being in the exact same place
as i was always meant for
like we could never miss out
for we had the whole world
right there in our palms
and the thing is
you may travel in space
but not in time
we could go back to that place
but not that state of mind
and it terrifies me
that i might never
feel like that
again

how do you fly
when your world is an ocean

how do you breathe in water
when you have lungs
not gills
how do you swim
when you don't have fins
but wings
there are fast fish all around me
and they want me to stay with them
but i don't speak their language
and they cannot understand it
i am calling out for some
of my own kind
for other birds
with their long legs and silky feathers
to come find me
and bring me to a better place

i once buried a love
that was still breathing
so now i hold on
to everything
that is already dead

you're a hybrid
with rainbow skin
no matter where you go
you seem to fit in

once i admired you for it
now i see
how you could never be trusted
for you are nothing more
than an imitation
of your surroundings
a slick mirror
with only a reflection of true color

and i could never get to know
what constantly changes

i cannot love
what never stays

the memories are better
than you ever were

it's not you
that i'm holding on to
it's not even us
it's the idea of it all
the memories
i have glorified with the light
of hope and dreams
the images we created
taken straight from the movies
the soundtrack we played
that made the whole world stop
while we hit repeat
but it was nothing more
than that
a short and sweet fantasy
you are not
what i need
and one day you'll be nothing
but a faint memory

why was it so easy for you
to make it so hard for me?

this is something
i will never understand
how you can use love as a weapon
a means to win a game
that i never agreed to play
why waste your time
your money and your energy
wrapping me in your web
branding my heart with your name
if you never truly cared anyway
so please
tell me
were you thinking of someone else?
or were you just
heartless

is it a gift
a curse
or simply human nature
to be drawn to nothing
but all that has the power
to destroy me

my greatest enemy is my memory
for the past clings to me
like water running down my body
i cannot let it go
only try and let it be
for it has simply become
a part of me

nothing scares me
quite like irrelevance

i have finally risen to a place
where i feel proud
but the thing about getting what you want
is that you risk losing it again
i have no fears
but this
that i will one day drift back
into oblivion
to a place where i will shout
and only hear a whisper
where i will write my truths down
only to watch the ink dry out
i am scared of being covered in dust
like old books on the shelf
only kept for the memories
as they're written in an outdated language
that no one speaks anymore
i am terrified
that i will one day write
with no readers
except for my own empty heart

the ocean

time knows no mercy

i wish to think of time
as my friend
that things come
and go in a way
that will make sense
in the end
that the clocks are working
in my favor
for all the right things
to finally come together
but the minutes keep passing
the hours keep slipping
out of my hands
i am sick of waiting
and my love is trembling
for bad timing has hurt me more
than any lover ever could

you loved me in waves
that's why i drowned

every now and then
i have a dream
of lining up every person
that i have ever harmed
those who walk around
with blood scars and broken bones
marked with my name
i wish i could see them again
to apologize for all that i did
to explain that it had nothing
to do with them
to finally admit
how sorry i am that i hurt you
with no reason but one:
a failed attempt to hide the fact
that i was already broken

maybe when the time is right
you will find me again

they say that
the best is yet to come
but i cannot imagine
anything as good
as being around you
so i choose to believe
that all good things
come to those who wait
everything is moving
and turning around with time
so maybe
things could change in a way
that brought our souls
in alignment again
after all
hope is the last thing to die
and i think that mine
is immortal

the silence has much to say

at last
everything is quiet
the dust from an invisible war
is settling
and in the empty space of air
under the weight of nothing
in the silence
do we hear
what we've been forgetting
the stories our bodies and the earth
have been trying to tell
for the silence speaks louder
than our words ever did
the truth is so crystal clear
no noise can whisk it away
and so this is my quiet prayer
that even when the air
is filled again
may we never forget
how to listen

i will forever remember the romance
we never had

you were never mine
but that will not stop me
from keeping you in my heart
the fictive touches
the air kisses
and all the imaginary moments
will always be mine
to return to
when i'm feeling lonely
for this is what i know
the timing was wrong
but i was not
and you will always be the best lover
i never had

once you go deep enough
the only light
you can truly rely on
is your own

i want to fall in love
to enter into a fantasy
i've had since i was little
but i don't
for i know by falling in love
i give someone the power
to destroy me
just when i've become whole

if i look back
will our eyes meet?

in my weak moments
i remember
what we did and
who we used to be
all the little details
that i'm fighting to forget
despite the small reminders
that i find everywhere
and i also wonder
if you sometimes do the same
for when we cannot meet
in reality
maybe we can meet
in the memories

your shell is a cage
not a home

it's not hard to tell
you were once more
than you tend to let on
you long for the past
for a time
when you didn't have to watch your back
before the pain and the treachery
when trusting the world around you
was only natural
now you live in your shell
behind walls of smiles and hollow words
living at a distance
where nothing can touch you
but what you don't see
is that when you shut others out
you imprison yourself within
for when you refuse to feel
the pain
the joy leaves with it
and you are left with a rib cage
full of nothing

i am desperate to hold on
to my youth
the freedom and the spontaneity
of drifting aimlessly around
careless and light on worries
for i am not done
i missed too much of it
crushed under the weight of my own pressure
lost in heavy thoughts and broken moments
crying for things
that had no greater meanings
blaming myself for all the mistakes
that i was meant to make
feeling like my life had ended
when it had barely begun

and now that i have found
my way back to life
i am terrified to find
that everyone else
has already moved on

what hurts more
is not the depression
it's the time i lost
fighting it

my heart is a child
it doesn't understand endings

my heart is always longing
reaching from my ribs
and asking for things
i can no longer give
how do i explain
that in this world
family turns into strangers
forests become deserts
and flames freeze to death
in less than an instant
how do i explain
that everything changes
even minds
even hearts
even things that once seemed
so real and eternal
tell me
how do i explain things
i don't understand myself?

invisibility is the only true freedom

sometimes i envy the air
for its ability to go anywhere
without anyone seeing
sometimes i wish i was the wind
so i didn't have to listen
to all that they're saying
sometimes i'm jealous of gray
for it does not have
to live up to any expectations
no matter how hard i try
to break out of the cage
of their minds
i find myself stuck in the same patterns
wishing to be lighter
stripped of all color
for when you're invisible
out of their reach
you're also
invincible
finally free

everything comes in waves

this world is an ocean
deep
complicated
and ever-changing
everything comes and goes
with the rhythm of waves
sometimes violently
crashing down on us
sometimes so softly
that we hardly notice
but we feel it
for whenever we try to hold on
to a person
a place
an emotion
it slips through our hands
just like water
and in those moments
when we realize
that nothing lasts forever
it's an art to keep our heads
above water

she is a mermaid
with wings in her mind
she will never be content in the ocean
or safe in the sky
so you will find her floating
on the surface
singing a slow song
of magic wishes and impossible dreams
with stars reflected in her eyes
and scales shimmering with moonlight
heart filled with envy
of both the birds high above her
and the fish deep beneath her
for when you are both
you are also
neither

hold on to nothing
but yourself

this life is a river
and you are the water
flowing with time
on your journey
back to the ocean
where you once came from
touching everything so lightly
until you leave it behind
you are meant for movement
not to be held back
by anything or anyone
moving in another direction
you're too soft
for any lasting attachment
there are forces
more powerful than you and me
that control our drifting
it will take
everything from you
except yourself

even a right love can go wrong

i like to think on love as stories
a book that we write
with our bodies as inked feathers
dancing around on days as paper
to create a fairy tale ending
but even the best of intentions
can sometimes break a good thing
even if everything else is right
one wrong word is enough
for the whole thing to fall apart
and for a plot twist
to change the genre
it's the risk of loving
that either it's forever
or it ends in tragedy
but whatever the outcome
there is no reason good enough
to ever stop writing

she looked at me
eyes wet with salt
asking
why is it so hard?
and i said
your waters are too rough
you must be kinder to yourself
how else could you survive the storm
when it's inside your head?

it's such a fine line
between feeling everything
and nothing at all

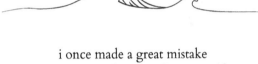

i once made a great mistake
that sent me far away from myself
it was an act of doubt
a betrayal of my own soul
for even though a heard a clear voice within
i chose to trust everyone else
thinking they knew another truth
that they would make the right choice
and i know what they did
was out of love
but no one will ever know me
like my own spirit do
and the path i choose
is only mine to walk
and so i found myself more lost
than i ever thought possible

i crossed the red desert
until i reached the edge of the world
where i found the sea
i stripped myself bare
broken down to the bone
and prayed for an answer
i begged the sun to show me light
pleaded the wind to show me a direction
until i finally turned around
and asked the ocean
who will save me?
and it whispered
again and again
yourself
yourself
yourself

not all empty spaces have to be filled

whoever or whatever
left a hole in your heart
does not necessarily need to be replaced
don't fight too hard
to fit something new
into what once was
these gaps of nothing
are needed in your life
as well as in music
in speeches
in art
for the deepfelt pauses
and breathtaking breaks
are not only beautiful themselves
they also prepare us for
whatever comes next

i write stories in the sand
the waves wash my letters away
and i begin again

-*the writer's curse*

imagine an empty bottle
floating around
surrounded by salt water
slipping through its cracks
finding the weak spots in the glass
and slowly filling it up
it must empty itself
or it will eventually drop
to the bottom of the sea
where no light will ever reach

imagine that
the next time you tell someone
to hold back their tears

the solitude is what i always come back to

i have always found it difficult
to be around people for too long
always on guard
for i will never know
how they think
and why they love
no place is more turbulent
than another human heart
and so i find myself coming back
again and again
to the peace and quiet of my own mind
the bottom of my soul
is mine alone
i am held by the things that i love
the music and the art
the words that i will never write
no matter how far i wander
i will call it home
for i can always come back to it
no matter how broken
i become

expect nothing
but the changes

let your thoughts be soft
and fluid like water
calm enough to settle wherever
to always find a rest
even when things change
but wild enough to transform
to freeze
to evaporate
and come together again as rain
rising and falling with the seasons
for even though nothing is certain
the change is
and we cannot prepare
for what is coming
without counting on surprises
once you let go
of the need for control
and start seeing the twists and turns
as messages from the universe
you will finally fall naturally
into your right place

the peace is in the future
not the past

i've been holding lost time in my hands
for too long
i no longer knows
what really happened
and what was merely
created in my own mind
i have been picking the past apart
to find every wrong point
in an attempt to never
make the same mistakes again
i have put the pieces together
in a million different ways
only to torture myself with the idea
of what it could have all meant
until this very day
where i decide to put it to rest
to open my hands to new blessings
and finally let all that happened
to them and to me
be

i was given a water heart
it never knows how to decide

of course i am scared
i am terrified by the depths
of diving down into the unknown
to find myself lost
in the darkest corners of my soul
confused and all alone
and i am unnerved
by the truths i might find
for once it's done
there is no coming back
to a place of innocence

but what scares me even more
is the thought of living my whole life
in the shallows

even mermaids must come up for air

we are hybrids
old souls in a modern world
half mortal and half gods
and sometimes we are torn
between what we need
and what we want
for we were made
for a life in waves
the constant changes
in our surroundings and in ourselves
with a blue mind
meant for deep conversation
yet the wind seems
to be calling our names
but our bodies are in need
of the oxygen
so remember to listen
to take a break
and come up for air
before it's too late

you deserve a lover made of pearls
i am sorry
you must empty oceans
to find it

- *the one*

whether you are in the storm
or in the silence
riding the top of the wave
or crawling on the bottom
never forget
how things change
sometimes even
within a moment

you are an ocean
in a desert world

you are a mosaic
of depths and waves
you are full of will
energy and power
but you hide it in a soft form
that is quite unusual
in this harsh world
and the thing is
these surroundings will make you feel
uncomfortable and wrong
for the dry desert land
does not know
how to handle passion storms
but you should know
that you are water
always complete
always whole
and you have so much to give
to this empty world

nothing is lost
until you give it up

luck is a fickle thing
coming and going in an invisible pattern
sometimes we worship the sky
for sending rains of blessings
other times we curse the world
for not giving what we need
but what my father taught me
is that whatever you're fishing for
the only way to catch anything
is if you try
each and every day
if you rise with the sun every morning
and get out on the water
even when the odds are against you
even if it all seems hopeless
the world will one day
give all your effort and trust back
but it cannot pour fortunes
into closed hands

i bottle all my emotions up
and pour them out on paper

i am a living breathing being
in an atmosphere of change
the ground under my feet
is spinning
the higher forces above me
are burning
and i feel the water within
being called to the moon
i could never be stable
for i change with the winds
and the seasons
i am too much a part
of this world
to ever be in control

sometimes the wrong choice
takes you to the right place

i know you've been wondering
twisting and turning recent events
to figure out
where it all went wrong
but even if you made mistakes
those are just small steps
on this magnificent path
and they are all here
for a reason
to take you somewhere else
so have faith
even when you think you're messing up
or going wrong
for sometimes only a bad choice
will get you to a good place

you are not your emotions

emotions are powerful
running through our bodies like electricity
changing our chemistry
but they are only temporary
and you are more
than what they say you are
maybe they differ like waves
but you remain like the ocean
where they are light rays
you are the sun itself
so even if your feelings seem flawed
unstable
or even broken
it doesn't mean that you are
you are allowed to feel
whatever is coming to you
and you are also allowed
to never let it define you

the only immortality i will ever have
is in what i create

this is both how and why i write
for i am branded by a desire
to create something
less fragile
and more timeless than me
to reach beyond my lifespan
and touch souls of future humans
for them to find comfort in my words
the same way i have had
millions of conversations
with those who came many years before me
even if i cannot stay
i want to create something that will
for forever may be impossible
but i will defy the odds
with my words
i have proved it
again and again
stories cannot be killed
not even once their writer
is eternally still

the ocean

pauses serve a purpose

somehow we have created expectations for
ourselves
that no one could ever live up to
we are humans
not machines
yet we push harder
to be productive all the time
as if we need to create
in order to be worthy
but just as no fire can keep burning
we cannot keep running
without eventually falling
so please do not carry regret or shame with you
when you retract for a while
it's perfectly alright
that you need space and time
to come back
twice as bright

the earth is seventy percent water
and so am i
oceans binding it all together
like the blood running
in my veins
and when i place my hands in the water
i try to remember
that just like me
the world is one

when i die
will you spread my ashes
in the ocean
take me home
so that i can be with you
wherever and whenever
you need me to

your mind is an endless masterpiece
if you allow it to be

it is a challenging truth
that every mind is designed
by the owner of it
for when it becomes a prison
we feel like victims
helpless to the shackles of shadows
but just as everything else finds new forms
so can the inside of your head
you decide what you allow
to enter it
your spirit has a unique way
of outgrowing itself
of shedding what is no longer relevant
of adding layers of consciousness
until it's a blooming bouquet
of truths both given and learned
of who you once were
and all you will become
it may be heavy at times
but once you open it up
your mind is the most magnificent art
of it all

maybe all i need to do now
is step back
and let it fix itself

trusting what we cannot see
only feel
is not easy
but the universe is so powerful
the energies speak the truth
and sometimes things work out
in a way we least expect them to
so even though it's in our nature
to try and control
everything
maybe this time
the right thing to do
is nothing

we have a whole world
that they will never know

that's the thing about love
it doesn't change your world
it creates a new one
for you to live in
a private haven
for a few carefully chosen
such a beautiful thing
to simply not care for anything else
for nothing else exists
the summer is in your touch
the wind is your voice
and i find myself
swimming in your eyes
there is no ecstasy
quite like the first days
of a romance
and no matter what happens
from now on
they could never take these moments
from us

she is all i ever wanted to be
complicated, deep, independent
wild and eccentric
but most of all
free

my tears are not a cry for help
but how i rinse my soul
it's not a sign of weakness
it's a natural process
of release
it's how i wash the day off
how i forgive those who did me wrong
it is my strength
for it allows me
to move on

nothing would be the same without you

there are days
where your existence feels like less of a gift
you feel the burden of irrelevance
wondering what you are here for
asking if anyone cares
but even if you feel small
frail and fragile
know that you are a crucial piece
in the most magnificent and complex
system the world has ever seen
your importance cannot be measured
for it is hidden in coincidences
you will touch hundreds of lives
that you will never feel
and gift thousands of smiles
that you will never see
you change the world
by living in it
and even when you are weak
your influence is unlimited

you're a constant
in my world of changes

the things in this world
are so light
they drift with the wind
rise and fly away
when the weather changes
everything is carried and controlled
by higher powers
even people
but you're a rock
grounding me in reality
your love is solid enough
for me to hold on to
so wherever i end up
whatever hits me
i know you'll be there
with me
and there's nothing more precious
than this
a constant
where nothing is certain

the beauty of life is the fragility of it

it intrigues me
how this world is so frail
a delicate balance between
powerful forces of life and death
that is so easily disturbed
we take time for granted
for we have never experienced
the end of it
but the only thing that is certain
is that it is coming
accidents happen in seconds
and right now
cancer cells could be spreading in your body
what matters right now
could be gone in the next moment
we build our lives so carefully
and conveniently forget
how easily things are broken
but i cannot help but think
that it is this uncertainty
that makes life so fascinating
and worth living

rain, rivers and streams
all that i have given
will come back to me

like salt water creates amber from resin
the waves of time will wash over you
again and again
shaping you into the person
you were meant to become

– *patience*

to be alive is a miraculous blessing
and it only lasts for a moment
i don't want to waste all my time
thinking
we are wild creatures
made to be free and spontaneous
to make this life
the greatest adventure
some days all i want to do
is leave my clothes and my worries behind
to run through the landscape
with an empty mind
and a hand in mine
to dance with the waves
instead of drowning in them
why are we obsessed
with achieving all these things
that mean nothing
on the day we die
why do we push and force
when we could just
enjoy

like the ocean
you can be everything at once

you are made of salts and water
emotional depth
and waves of thoughts
you are just like the ocean
with all of its facets
deadly
but so full of life
soft and humble
but also forceful
constant
but always in motion
independent
but still reflecting the surroundings
simple and reachable
but so full of mystery
just like salt water waves
you weren't meant
to fit in boxes
you don't have to be
either or
for you can be both
and more

from the start of my world
i have been an ocean overflowing
i used to pour my soul
into every mind i met
only to be broken by the fact
that it could not contain me
that no one would ever understand
until i found traces of salt
in the books on my shelves
and i started writing my own words
on pages instead of lips
that was when
you found me
with a heart deep and open enough
to hold all that i am
thank you for listening
thank you for giving me a place
to finally exist
limitlessly

-to my reader

acknowledgements

to my father
for sharing your love for the ocean
and teaching me the art of being soft

to all my oceans
those who embraced my depths
when i was at my lowest

to you
for flowing with me
to change the world
not with force
but with consistency

about the author

Kamilla Tolnø is a danish writer and dreamer.
her entire life has been led by her love for lan-
guage and the art of writing. apart from working
several years as a copywriter she has published a
danish short story collection in 2017.

she has created and shared minimalistic poetry
and illustrations on her social media channels for
years, reaching readers all across the globe.

the northern collection is her debut as an interna-
tionally renown poet. growing up amongst pine
trees and snowflakes inspired her to name this
collection after her place of origin.

apart from writing her soul burns for travel and
arts. and she wishes to experience it all with her
heart open and eyes closed.

more art on ktolnoe.com
or social media @k.tolnoe

the northern collection

the ocean is the third of four books in *the northern collection*. a manifestation of the internal journey that we must all face at some point in our lives; the journey to our true north.
to our home.

the true north is a place that's different to every-one. it's the place where all the energetic lines meet. where we find answers and find peace. for we cannot help the world until we help ourselves.

the northern collection is most of all a place to unite. to grow. to heal. to become. together.
i invite you to share any thoughts, feelings or dreams you may have with me. for us to come to-gether as a community. and to serve as inspiration for the next books and steps to come.

join the conversation on ktolnoe.com
or social media channels @k.tolnoe

CPSIA information can be obtained
at www.ICGtesting.com
Printed in the USA
LVHW010007150822
725931LV00004B/758